Grades 1-3

DATE DUE

A Zoo for You

Some Indoor Pets
and How to Keep Them

By WINIFRED and CECIL LUBELL

Parents' Magazine Press · New York

A STEPPING-STONE BOOK

CONTENTS

19770

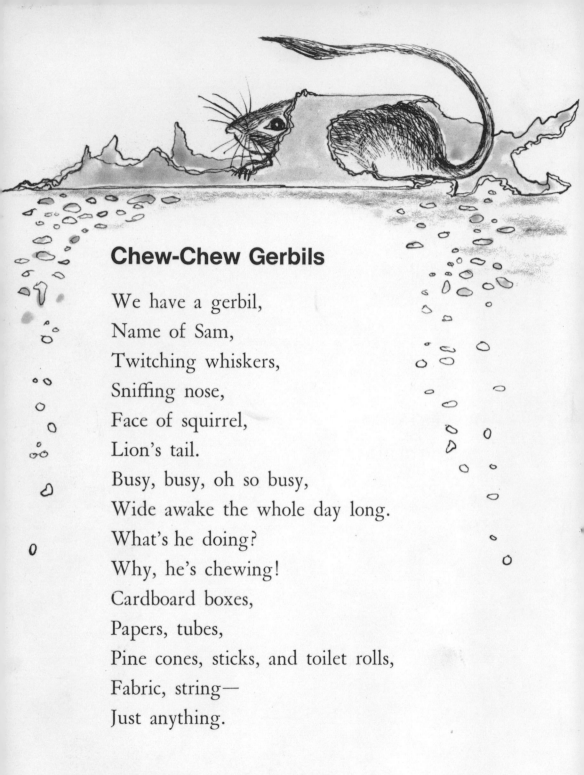

Chew-Chew Gerbils

We have a gerbil,
Name of Sam,
Twitching whiskers,
Sniffing nose,
Face of squirrel,
Lion's tail.
Busy, busy, oh so busy,
Wide awake the whole day long.
What's he doing?
Why, he's chewing!
Cardboard boxes,
Papers, tubes,
Pine cones, sticks, and toilet rolls,
Fabric, string—
Just anything.

He's rushing here, rushing there,
Up the ladder, down the ladder,
Scooting through the tin-can tunnel,
Eight fast laps around the wheel.
Then he stops,
Then looks around,
Then back to chewing,
Always chewing.
We thought him lonely,
Got him Sue.
Oh yes, she's quite a chewer too.
Five weeks later she had babies,
Three of them,
All hairless pink.
Two months more and they were grown.
And now all five are busy, busy;
They've turned their house into a factory—
All day working,
Hardly ever still,
A Chew-Chew Gerbil Chewing Mill.

5

What Is a Gerbil?

A gerbil is a lively little animal that belongs to the same family as the mouse. It looks like a mouse, but it's a little bigger.

How can you know it isn't a mouse? Very easy. Its fur is much thicker and its tail is more furry. Also, its back legs are much longer than its front legs—like a kangaroo.

A full-grown gerbil weighs about three ounces. Its body is from three to four inches long, with a tail almost as long as its body.

The gerbil comes from hot, dry deserts in Africa, in China, and in Russia. It was first brought to America in 1955 for laboratory experiments. Since then it has become a popular pet, and now you can buy gerbils in most pet stores.

For a Gerbil House

A gerbil is a desert animal so it needs to be warm. Keep it in a warm place, away from drafts, and it should stay healthy.

The best kind of house is a fish tank with a wire screen on top. Even an old, leaky one will do. A metal cage with an exercise wheel is also good. You can buy them in pet stores.

A cardboard or wooden box will *not* do, because the gerbil will soon gnaw its way out. That's why you need wire screening on top of your tank. This also will keep your pet safe from cats.

Put wood chips down on the floor of your gerbil house. Put in cloth, string, or cotton wool. It will tear them up into a fluffy pile for a bed.

Housecleaning is easy. A gerbil doesn't smell. Just change the bedding and wash the floor with soap and water every three weeks.

For a Gerbil Playground

Here are some good play toys for a gerbil:

A cardboard roll from toilet paper;

An empty toothpaste box;

A small open tin can;

These all make good tunnels.

A wire ladder;

Wood blocks for climbing;

Exercise wheels for running.

Give your gerbils a small cereal box and they will tear it to shreds in half an hour.

Above all, play with your gerbils so they get used to being handled.

Try putting one in your pocket.

For Gerbil Food

Gerbils don't overeat, so you can always keep the food dish full. Give them any of these foods:

Bird seed

Uncooked cereal, such as oatmeal

Dry cereal, such as corn flakes

Dog biscuits, broken up

Rice, uncooked

Apple, carrot, lettuce, celery

Hamster food, sold in pet stores

Bits of dried toast

Our gerbils also like sunflower seeds and they love raw spinach. What do yours like best?

Gerbils don't need much water because they come
from the desert where it's dry. They get water
from vegetables, but we also give them a small dish
of water. Fill the dish with pebbles so they don't
knock it over. You can also use an upside-down
water bottle with a tube. Pet stores sell them.

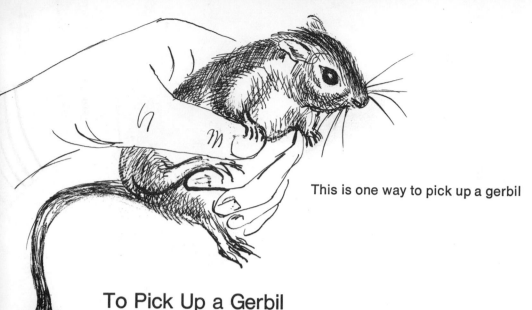

This is one way to pick up a gerbil

To Pick Up a Gerbil

A gerbil is very curious. Usually it will walk onto the palm of your hand and you can scoop it up. Be careful not to squeeze it. If it won't come to you, pick it up by its tail, close to the body.

Don't ever grab a gerbil from above. It will get frightened and run away.

Put your hand in the cage for a few minutes every day. Pick it up and stroke it.

Some gerbils bite at first, especially if there's a cat nearby to make them nervous. To tame them, you need to handle them every day. We found the best thing to do was to wear leather gloves while we fed them sunflower seeds, which they like.

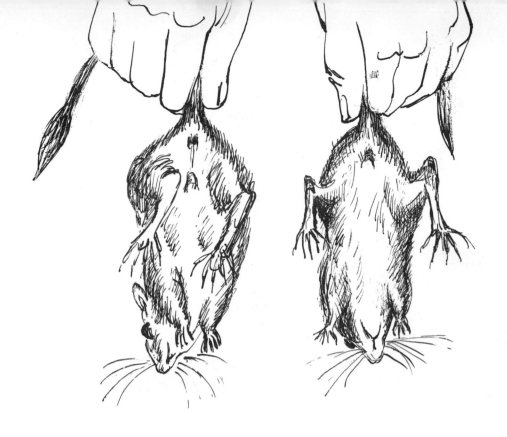

You can tell a male (*father*) gerbil from a female (*mother*) because the male has a more pointed body and a small pouch on its belly near the tail.

Even so, gerbils look very much alike. To tell them apart we marked our male gerbil with shoe paint on the top of his head. This didn't last long, so we had to paint it over again every few weeks.

Newborn gerbil

One week old

Two weeks old

Six weeks old

Gerbil Babies

If you have a male (*father*) gerbil and a female (*mother*) you will probably have gerbil babies—three, four, or five at a time.

The newborn gerbils look like pink piglets, about an inch long.

Don't touch them until they grow up and open their eyes. This takes about three weeks.

And don't play with the mother or father until the babies have grown up. It will make them nervous and they may bite you.

A gerbil snuggle

Gerbil Questions

Our male gerbil makes a drumming sound on the floor with his hind legs. Does yours? We think he does this as a warning to the other gerbils when our cat comes too close. What do you think?

Our gerbils get very excited when we give them dry pine cones to gnaw. What do yours like best for gnawing?

How small a hole can your gerbils get through? Try them with holes in a cardboard box.

Our gerbils get bored with old toys. Yours will, too. What new toys can you think of for them?

A Squeaky Hamster

Our hamster was a baby when he came.
We called him Squeaky
For the noise he made.
Each time we put a hand into his cage
He scurried to a corner,
Letting out a howl of slurpy squeaks.
And if we tried to stroke him—
What a fuss!
That three-inch bit of orange fur
Rolled over on his back,
Put up his paws,
Was going to fight us! Yes, he was!

Well, now he's older;
Now he's used to us.
He's much, much calmer than our gerbils.
He cuddles in a corner nest,
Curled into a furry ball.
And when we put a hand in,
Out he comes to play.
He loves to have his belly scratched,
And if he gets a peanut,
He takes it gently in his soft pink paws,
Then sits up straight to eat it,
Looking like a small toy bear.

You can recognize a hamster
By the stubby little tail
And by the puffed-out cheeks.
There are pockets in its cheeks
For storing food
Until it's ready for a meal.
It eats the same things that a gerbil eats
And wants a house just like a gerbil house.
You'll need to clean the cage out once a week
Or it will smell.
And when you clean the hamster's house,
Throw out the wood chips,
But be sure to put the bedding back.
It's quite a job to make a whole new bed.

A Gentle Guinea Pig

The guinea pig we got was all grown up.
How big he looked!
He seemed at least three times as big
As our pet hamster or our gerbil, Sam.
And that's not counting tails.
The guinea pig
Just doesn't have a tail at all.
We made a house for him,
A big one from a wooden box—
A screen for the front,
Some straw for the floor,
And a sign on the door
Saying: "Beware the Wild Boar."

A boar is a male pig,
But that's a joke,
For he's the gentlest creature in our zoo:
Won't bite, won't scratch,
Won't gnaw on wood,
Won't jump or climb,
No fuss, no smell,
And where you put him, he stays put.
He does make squealy noises like a pig
But actually, he's not a pig at all.
He's called a *Cavy* by the scientists,
And often he is used by them
To test the way new medicines will work.

Our guinea pig eats quite a lot.
He gets raw vegetables twice a day:
Green lettuce, spinach, celery tops,
A piece of carrot, sometimes apple, too,
As well as other foods—
The dry ones that a hamster likes.
We leave a water bottle in his box,
And clean his house out once a week.
A guinea pig needs very little care.

We sometimes say
That *people* have been used as guinea pigs.
What does that mean?

In summer our guinea pig
eats grass and dandelion leaves

Three Bright Mice

Our neighbor, John, is eight years old
And we are baby sitters for his two brown mice,
Happy and Snappy—
Two boys, he told us.
Their bedroom is a small tin can.
Their bed is made of cotton balls
Which they have pulled inside the can.
All day,
Until the sun goes down,
They disappear inside their fluffy bed.
Then promptly,
Every night at 8 o'clock,
Out comes Happy,
Poking his nose out through the cotton balls.

Whiskers twitching,
Black eyes darting,
First he looks to right and left,
Then above, and then behind.
"All's clear!"
And out he pops
With Snappy right behind his tail.
They scoot to every corner of the cage.
They climb the ladder,
Whirl the wheel,
Then sit down to clean themselves—
A careful scrubbing,
Every hair,
Top and bottom,
Front and back,
All along the long brown tail.
Then the face is scrubbed by foot,
Then the feet,
And they are done—
And very neatly done at that.

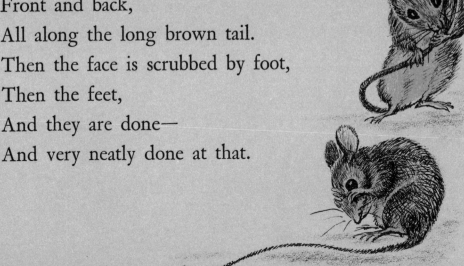

But one night
Only Happy came at 8.
What, no Snappy!
Where is he tonight?
We look.
We turn the bedroom can on end.
Yes, there he is!
But *he's* no *he*,
For sliding out are three of them—
Snappy and two pink hairless baby mice
No bigger than your finger nail.
Oh, John was wrong!
A big mistake!
They weren't two boys at all, at all!

John's friend Kathy has a mouse—
A white one, name of Jennifer.
Not like the brown ones,
She's awake all day.
She's very tame,
Eats from your hand,
Sometimes runs right up your arm,
May sit on your shoulder
Nibbling a seed.
And what an acrobat is she!
She climbs the ladder,
Jumps from there,
Grabs the wire with her pink front paws,
Then walks around the cage—
But upside down,
Like a fly on the ceiling.
A private circus, that's what Kathy has.

Wild Mice & Tame Mice

Wild mice are brown or gray with hairy tails. They live in woods and fields and have big eyes for seeing in the dark. That's because they come out of their nests only at night.

John's two pets are wild ones called *Deer Mice,* with white feet and bellies. He caught them in a nest in the woods and is taming them.

Tame mice, like Kathy's, have smaller eyes and hairless tails. They are all related to the gray *House Mouse.* You can find them in at least 70 different colors. Kathy's mouse is white all over and has pink eyes.

A Mouse Menu

Mice live mostly on seeds and vegetables. Here is a good daily menu for one mouse. If you have two mice, double the amount.

Monday, Wednesday, Friday: 1 teaspoon bird seed; 1 teaspoon bread soaked in milk.

Tuesday, Thursday, Saturday: 1 teaspoon oatmeal; 1 teaspoon rice. Both uncooked.

Sunday: Special treat—1 small dog biscuit, two raisins, and a peanut.

Every Day: Fresh water. Small bits of carrot, lettuce, celery, cabbage. Also a small piece of wood or a small bone for gnawing.

Note 1: No cheese. No meat. It makes them fat.

Note 2: Try other foods, such as cornflakes.

For a Mouse House

The best house for more than one mouse is a
ten-gallon fish tank. It keeps out drafts and is
easy to clean. For *one* mouse, a metal cage with
an exercise wheel is very good. A big glass jar
will also do quite well.

If you use a fish tank or a jar always put a wire
screen on top—to keep your mice *in* and other
animals *out,* especially the cat, if you have one.
It will also protect your pets from wild rats or
wild mice who may get into your house.

Mice clean themselves a lot but they don't clean their house. You must do that for them or it gets very smelly.

Every day, take out the food they haven't eaten. Once a week, empty the whole cage and wash it.

To do this, put the mice in a separate jar. You can pick them up by their tails or catch them in a small can and drop them into the jar. Be careful they don't escape!

Mouse House Furniture

Wood chips for the floor.

A food dish and a water bottle.

An empty tin can for a bedroom.

Cotton wool, paper, and string for a bed.

Toys, such as a ladder, a seesaw, a swing, and especially an exercise wheel.

Mouse Families

Keeping a male and a female mouse as pets is interesting but also very difficult because they have lots of babies—so many, you won't know what to do with them.

It goes this way: after they mate, it takes only three weeks for the babies to be born. There may be six or eight of them, sometimes more.

They are born pink and hairless but they grow hair in two or three days and they open their eyes in two weeks. In only two months these new mice will be ready to have their own babies.

This goes on and on every two months, and mice usually live from two to three years if they are healthy. So you can see there would be too many mice in your house in a very short time.

It's better to get two males, or two females. Don't mix them and you won't have baby mice. Of course, you may make a mistake, as John did. It's hard to tell a male mouse from a female.

So, if you *do* get mouse babies unexpectedly, this is what you must do: take the father mouse out of the cage for two weeks until the babies are grown. Otherwise, sad to say, he may eat them.

Questions

How many toes does a mouse have on its back feet? How many on its front feet?

A Turtle or Two

Our turtles *look* a lot alike,
But they don't *act* alike at all.
The smaller one is sleepy slow.
It hides all day beneath a stone,
And if we put it on the floor,
It will not budge.
It just plays dead.
At first it would not eat a thing
Until we found a food it liked.
And what was that?
A piece of cheese, if you please!

The bigger one is full of pep.
It crawls around.
It takes a swim.
And every day at 5 o'clock
It sits there waiting for its dinner.
It pokes its head out from its shell,
Blinks its tiny slits of eyes,
Snaps the food up with its beak,
Tears it with its two front feet,
And then looks up as though to say:
"Yes, that was very, very good."
For exercise we put it on the floor.
Quick as a wink it swings around
And scurries for the wall.
Who said a turtle must be slow?
Not so!

What Is a Turtle?

A turtle is a reptile. So is a snake, a lizard, and a crocodile. Like all these creatures, a turtle is cool when you touch it.

That's because it has cool blood. Other animals —and people too—have warm blood. Their blood stays at about the same temperature all the time, unless they get sick and have a fever.

But the blood of a reptile doesn't stay at the same temperature. It changes with the outside temperature. In a cold room it simply goes to sleep. That's why you must keep a turtle warm if you want it to be lively.

A turtle breathes with lungs like other land animals but can stay under water a long time.

It has a hard beak, like a bird, and no teeth.

Our two turtles are called *Red-eared Sliders* because they have a red stripe behind each eye.

The tops of their shells are green and the bottoms are yellow with black designs. These designs are different for each turtle, just as fingerprints are different for each person.

Right now, our turtles are about two inches long because they are only a few months old. But if we take good care of them they will grow to eight inches in a few years.

For a Turtle House

Our *Red-ears* need land to crawl on and water to swim in.

We made a good house for them out of a big food container with high sides. It's twelve inches long and eight inches wide.

We covered the bottom with a layer of fine gravel—about one inch thick. That makes it easy for them to crawl around and dig holes.

On top of the gravel we poured about an inch of water for them to swim in.

Then we gave them two or three flat stones to help them crawl out of the water. They also like to dig holes under the stones and hide there.

We keep our turtle house partly in the sunshine for an hour or two every day. A turtle needs sun just as we do. If you can't do that, put a small electric light over the house.

In the winter we keep our turtle house near a radiator where it's warm.

Turtle Food

We feed our turtles a little food every day at about 5 o'clock.

They eat tiny pieces of raw meat, or fish, or chicken—all chopped up fine. Some days we give them dried shrimp flakes or a crumb of cheese. And we always leave a small piece of lettuce in their tank.

Our smaller turtle will only eat food that is floating on top of the water. The bigger one only eats under water.

We change the water every two days because it gets smelly with old food.

Turtle Games

Turtles need exercise.

We pick ours up carefully by the sides of their shells so we don't squeeze them. Then we put them down on the floor to race each other to the wall. The big one always wins, but the smaller one is beginning to crawl a little faster now.

Sometimes we build a maze with blocks or dominoes. They always find their way out easily.

Don't Get a Painted Turtle

Painting a turtle's shell is very bad. It keeps the shell from growing and might even kill the poor turtle.

If someone gives you a painted turtle, ask an older person to clean the paint off with turpentine or nail-polish remover. It has to be done very carefully so as not to touch the turtle's eyes.

Questions About Turtles

If your turtle lands on its back will it be able to turn itself over?

How long can your turtles stay under water?

Why do you think a turtle has to use its feet to tear up its food?

Can you see where we got the idea for turtleneck sweaters?

Some Quiet Goldfish

The men who dive beneath the sea
Have called the sea a silent world.
They see the fish go swimming by;
They watch the crawlers moving
On the bottom of the sea—
And there are trillions of them,
Many more than anyone can count—
But never do the divers hear a sound.
Our own aquarium is just like that—
A silent world, although a very little one.

Our fish are goldfish,
Four of them,
All orange-red and gold,
All Fantails,
Swimming in a silent row,
Between the cool green water plants,
Around the gray-green rocks,
Then gliding down
To nudge the gravel on the floor,
Then shooting upward
With their waving tails and fins,
Then down again and past the snails
Who stick like peanut butter to the glass,
And all without the slightest sound;
So quietly,
It's like a movie when the sound goes dead.

Our young friend Jan has goldfish too.

"They make me think of birds," he says.

"They wave their fins

As though they're flying slowly in the air."

And what does Jan like most about his fish?

"I like to watch them as I fall asleep," he says.

What Does a Goldfish Need?

A goldfish is like other fish. It belongs to the family of fish called *carp*.

It needs water to swim in—the more the better.

It needs food to eat—but very little.

It needs air to breathe. Does that surprise you? We'll explain.

How a Fish Gets Air

All creatures need air in order to live. That is, they need the oxygen in the air. People need it too. We get it by breathing air into our lungs. But a fish can't breathe air. It has to take oxygen from the water.

All water has some oxygen, and a fish can take the oxygen out of the water with its gills. The gills are underneath the flaps which every fish has on the sides of its head.

When you see a goldfish gulping water with its big mouth, it's not drinking. It's breathing. The water passes over its gills and out through the flaps, leaving the oxygen behind.

That's why you must make sure that the water in your aquarium has enough oxygen. There are four ways to do this:

1. *By having a big tank.* The surface of the water gets oxygen from the air. The bigger the surface, the more oxygen it gets.

2. *By having green water plants in the tank.* As the plants grow, they give off oxygen. For this you need sand on the bottom to hold the plants.

3. *By changing the water twice a week.* The new water will have more oxygen. You don't need to do this if you have plants. If you *do* change the water, use a rubber tube (a siphon) so as not to disturb the fish.

4. *By using an electric bubbler.* It pumps air into the water. You don't need this either if the tank is big enough and has growing plants.

How Big a Tank?

You need one gallon of water for each fish one inch long, not counting tails. So, a two-inch fish needs two gallons of water.

If you have a ten-gallon tank like ours, you can keep four goldfish, each two inches long. Always leave extra room. The fish will grow and the tank is never filled up to the top.

A round glass bowl will also do. Fill it only to the widest part. Then it has a bigger water surface to take in more oxygen.

Keep It Clean

It's important to keep your aquarium clean. Take out the fish waste and old food before they spoil the water. You can do this easily with a glass tube sold in pet stores.

If the walls of your tank become cloudy, that's because tiny green plants called *algae* are growing there. This happens if the tank gets too much sun or electric light. You can scrape off the algae.

It's good to keep two or three snails in the tank. They eat some of the algae and some of the leftover food. And they're interesting to watch.

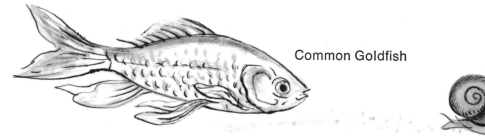

Common Goldfish

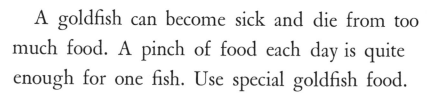

A goldfish can become sick and die from too much food. A pinch of food each day is quite enough for one fish. Use special goldfish food.

Comet

Fantail

Black Moor

Tropical Fish Are Not Goldfish

Goldfish and tropical fish are different kinds of fish and it's best not to mix them.

Tropical fish need much more care. They also need warm water, so the aquarium must have an electric heater.

Goldfish don't need as much care. They're stronger and live very well in cool water. In fact, full-grown goldfish can often live all winter under the ice in an outdoor pool.

Shubunkin

Quiet, Bud!

Come meet our parakeet.
We call him *Bud*.
I walk into the room, stand near his cage.
He starts to squawk.
He's scolding me.
We've been away the whole long day
And no one came to talk to him.
He's quite annoyed,
But still he's greeting me.

He knows I've brought him something good to eat.
I always do.
"All right," I say. "Now, quiet, Bud!"
He cocks his head at me and parrots back:
"Quiet, Bud! Quiet, Bud!"
The only words he knows.
It took him several months to learn them.
He repeats them all day long.
I open up his cage.
He hops out on my finger
And we take a walk around the room.
He flies off to the window,
Then comes back.
He perches on my shoulder, chattering:
"Quiet, Bud! Quiet, Bud!" and flaps his wings.

"What now?" I say. "What do you want?"
But I know very well he wants a treat.
I hold a piece of apple up.
He takes it gently with his beak.
"Not here!" I say, "you'll make a mess."
We walk back to his cage. He hops inside
And gobbles up his fruit.
"Thanks!" I say out loud, "Say thanks!"
He looks at me but doesn't say the word.
It's still too new and hard to learn.
But soon he will.
He's very bright.

A Parakeet Is a Budgie

We call our parakeet *Bud,* which is short
for *budgie.* And budgie is short for *budgerigar.*
That's the name for a parakeet in Australia, where
it came from originally. It means "pretty bird."

A parakeet looks like a small parrot, but it's
really a different kind of bird. You can tell it's
not a parrot because its shape is much thinner
and more pointed.

The feathers on our Bud are green and yellow.
He has a bright blue spot on each cheek. You can
find parakeets in many pretty colors, but they
almost always have those blue spots.

The skin just above Bud's beak is also blue.
That tells us he's a male. Female parakeets have
tan or brown skin above their beaks when they
are full-grown.

A Cage for Bud

We bought Bud a good big cage so he could get some exercise in his house. We got the unpainted kind because we knew he would bite off the paint.

The cage has a little platform outside so he can get back in easily. Inside it has two wooden perches, as well as a small tree branch. There is also a swing and two cups—one for food, and the other for water.

On the floor of his cage we've put gravel from the pet store. He eats a little of it because a parakeet has no teeth and the gravel helps him to digest his food.

Between the bars of his cage we tied a piece of cuttlebone which we bought in the pet store. He sharpens his beak on the bone and he also needs it to keep him healthy.

We stand the cage away from drafts and strong sunlight. At night we cover it with a big cloth. That helps him get to sleep.

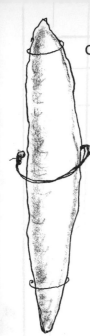

Clean-Up Day

With a parakeet, every day is clean-up day. But it takes only a few minutes.

We empty Bud's food and water cups every day. We wash them. Then we fill them up again.

Once a week—on Friday—we take out the tray on the bottom of the cage and wash it. Then we put down fresh gravel.

At the same time we scrape the perches clean with a knife. We don't use water for that because the perch should be rough, so he can grab it.

Friday is also bath day for Bud. We put a big saucer of water down on the floor of his cage. If we don't watch out, we get showered ourselves as he flaps his wings and chatters away.

Not all parakeets like baths, but our Bud does; we think he'd like it to be Friday every day.

Feeding Is Easy

It's no trouble to feed a parakeet.

We give Bud the special parakeet seed sold in pet stores. He gets a new dish full every day. He also gets a piece of lettuce or other fresh green vegetable every day.

Two or three times a week he gets a piece of apple, or pear, or banana. And once in a while we give him a pet-store treat, especially if he's learned a new word and we want to reward him.

We never give him sweets, or cake, or cookies. They would make him too fat.

Training Is Hard

It's not easy to train a parakeet but it's worth the trouble.

You should begin when it's young. We started to train Bud when he was three months old. At first he snapped at our fingers and we had to wear gloves until he learned to trust us.

We began by slowly putting a hand into his cage and offering him a treat, talking to him quietly all the time.

Later we got him to perch on our fingers inside
the cage. After a few weeks he let us take him in
and out of the cage on a finger. For this he got
a treat each time.

Teaching him a few words was more difficult. He
can learn only one word at a time—an easy one.
We keep repeating the word slowly for him, several
times a day, but especially when we cover his cage
at night and uncover it in the morning.

The most important thing we learned was to
move slowly so Bud would not get frightened.

Pet Watching

What do you notice when you watch your pets?

Do you think a parakeet understands words?
Or is it just repeating sounds?

How does a goldfish use its tail? For swimming?
Or only for steering?

How does a snail stick to a glass wall?

Can your turtles hear sounds?

Have you noticed that a hamster's front paws
look a lot like human hands?

Do all gerbils act the same? Or does each
behave differently, the way people do?

Ask yourself other questions about your pets and
see if you can find the answers.

You can learn a lot about animals just by
watching your pets, but you will probably forget
unless you write down what you see.

We keep a notebook for *our* pets. Each day we
write down the things they do and the things we
notice. Perhaps you'd like to do the same.

February 12
Turtle's shell harder.
little one's eyes o.k.
Hamster slept all day,
no nipping, ate apple.

Febuary 20.
lost turtle. cat? Found
it later under big chair.
was not hurt. Swam around
and ate.

cleaned gerbil's house. They
didn't like it. Quickly chewed
up egg box. gave them lots of
sunflower seeds + a carrot.

February 26.
Hamster much tamer.
Had him out on my shoulder.

March 2.
Hamster doesn't seem
afraid of cat or dog.
Must try with turtle.
climbs up. curtains—very
high.

March 4.
got a batch of pinecones
for gerbils.

61

Why Does a Pet Need Care?

It needs you to take care of it because it isn't living outdoors where it can take care of itself. When it lives indoors, in *your* house, or in your classroom, it needs *your* help to get food and water, and to keep clean.

So you can't just go away and leave it alone. If you *do* go away for more than a day, you need a pet-sitter. That's why our neighbor, John, asked us to take care of his mice when he went to visit his grandmother.

Something else, and this is very important.

When an animal lives in a cage, it can't run away from you if it's frightened, the way it could if it lived outdoors. So try not to frighten it.

Don't make sudden movements when you put your hand in its cage. If you move slowly and gently, it will soon learn to trust you.

Index